1401
Even More Things That

P*SS
Me Off

1401

Even More Things That

P*SS
Me Off

I. M. Peeved
and
Ed Strnad

Developed by
The Philip Lief Group, Inc.

A Perigee Book

Perigee Books
are published by
The Berkley Publishing Group
200 Madison Avenue
New York, NY 10016

Library of Congress Cataloging-in-Publication Data

Peeved, I. M.
    1401 even more things that p*ss me off / I.M. Peeved and
Ed Strnad; developed by the Philip Lief Group, Inc.
    p.   cm.
    ISBN 0-399-52123-2 (pbk. : acid free)
    I. Philip Lief Group. II. Title. III. Title: 1401 even more
things that p*ss me off. IV. Title: One thousand four hundred
and one even more things that p*ss me off.
PN6162.P354 1994   94-10197
818'.540208—dc20

Published by arrangement with The Philip Lief Group, Inc.
6 West 20th Street, New York, NY 10011

Printed in the United States of America
1 2 3 4 5 6 7 8 9 10

This book is printed on acid-free paper

Acknowledgments

The author peevishly acknowledges malcontented babysitter Lidia Hasenauer, long-suffering spouse JoAnn Strnad, disgruntled editor Gary Sunshine, and the ornery George Zarr.

Introduction

You wake up to the sun, feeling refreshed and full of energy. You grab a sinfully delectable doughnut, knowing it won't add a pound to your perfect body. You put on your terrific clothes, hop into your enviable sports car, and off you go, ready to report to your completely fulfilling, high-paying job. Your day progresses joyously as you find yourself immersed in the comfort of the same stress-free, collegial atmosphere you enjoy every day of the year—it's so perfect that you would never even think to take a vacation.

Can you imagine a life without complaints? What would we be like if we had no targets upon which to vent our ire, our venom, our choicest words? Content? Maybe. Satisfied? Perhaps. As bland as unflavored gelatin? Most definitely. To protect you from becoming chronically complacent, we've dipped into our simmering stewpot to serve you a heaping portion of *1401 Even More Things That P*ss Me Off*.

Venting the first 2,802 peeves should have gotten it all out of our systems, but as it turns out, the powers that be give us new things to complain about all the time, making a third volume inevitable. For instance, there's the new fad of resurrecting dead actors and forcing them to appear in cola commercials, and the flap over Hillary Rodham Clinton's name, or media coverage of severed body parts. Each day, we have moments of angry revelation, when we hear our inner voices screaming, "I can't live in a world with hardened gunk between the tines of forks . . . white flossing speckles on the bathroom mirror . . . computer keyboards incapacitated by spilled soda." And yet, we carry on, resilient and strong, as the universe continues to test our limits.

1401 Even More Things That P∗ss Me Off will provide you with a fresh supply of life's little treats. Use it to identify your sore spots and even develop new sources of anguish. After studying this book and its two predecessors, you'll never have to worry about feeling only vaguely irritated again, because you'll know exactly what you're up against: a world teeming with reasons to be peeved.

adults who had happy childhoods

theaters that charge extra for "butter
flavor" on your popcorn

the law against cruel and unusual
punishment

fiftysomething Beatles

the return of painfully thin fashion
models

when your pets never warn you of
  impending earthquakes

not having the Commies to pin all
  our paranoias on anymore

countdowns to the end of Clinton's
  presidency

chapped lips

that your cat doesn't give a damn if
  you live or die

billboards that track the national debt

people who call you only when they
    want something

indecipherable abbreviations in classi-
    fied ads

klutzes and yutzes

the stench behind a seafood restau-
    rant

the people who come out of the wood-
work to exploit your wealth when
you're rich and famous

that disgusting slime on canned hams

when graffiti is called art

former computer nerds who now refer
to themselves as cyberpunks

adults who wear baseball caps backwards

people who slurp their coffee, then
   say "Ahhh"

fifth-graders "packing iron"

non-ticklish people

junk mail that looks like it contains a
   real check

dog and cat owners who kiss their
   pets on the mouth

when you catch yourself thinking maybe Dan Quayle was right

new movies based on old TV shows

kids' TV shows based on action-figure toys or videogames

discovering mouse droppings inside your home

pasty-faced kids who stay indoors on sunny days

parents who force their kids to go see
    Santa

parents who take small children across
    the country in an airplane

Nixon's pardon

the petrified French fries that fell be-
    tween your car seats years ago

ninety-year-old bungee jumpers and
    sky divers

predictions about the future that never came true, like house-cleaning robots and rocket-powered cars

having no free time to use your "time-saving" appliances

psychotherapy's fifty-minute "hour"

psychotherapy's hourly rate

sushi haters who say that eating sushi reminds them of eating at a bait shop

people who can play tunes with their
     armpits, and are oddly proud
     of it

people who are waiting for California
     to fall into the ocean

spicy food so hot your lips and tongue
     burn for hours

trying to give your order to the dough-
     nut salesperson on the other side
     of the glass case

automatic seatbelts

when anesthesia wears off too soon

people who leave the price tag on
   presents

parents who walk their kids on a wrist-
   leash

smokers who drive with the windows
   rolled up and children in the car

the NRA

glasses that leave gory pinch marks on your nose

going to work with bits of bloody toilet tissue stuck on your face

people who expose a lot of "crack" when they squat

having to watch your friends' home video of their child's birth

discovering someone is making a fortune from an idea you mentioned offhandedly potato chips-in-a-can

dry cleaners who charge more to clean
    women's shirts

kids who eat paste

when your mom reminds you how
    many hours of labor she endured
    having you

wondering why Donald Trump is still
    living large when he's supposed
    to be broke

Cadillac owners who drive as if the road came as a supplied accessory

the flap over Hillary Rodham Clinton's name

babies who are being given surnames for first names (e.g.: Cooper, Skyler, etc.)

severed body parts in the news

people who boast "I don't even own a TV" but somehow know the rules for *Wheel of Fortune* when a black cat crosses your path

roller coaster riders who stick their arms up

being dubbed "Generation X" by the media

being unable to recite the alphabet without singing the little song

newspapers with blurry, misaligned color photos

when the tulips don't open

talking to someone who has one eye-
    brow that's much hairier than
    the other

babysitters who don't pick up the
    phone

ruining the design when you rip off a
    perforated tissue box lid

that cheated feeling if you were born
    around December 25th

seeing back-to-school ads in August

job applicants who start their interviews
by asking about the vacations

strangers who call you "Hon"

libraries with computers instead of
good old-fashioned card cata-
logues

when the only grocery carts available
are wet

people who examine their handker-
chiefs after blowing their noses

getting hassled for wearing white after
Labor day

people who believe that louder is
better for things like cars, tools,
and talking

why it's always a "disgruntled" postal
worker who snaps and goes ber-
serk

that there is a national Stop Smoking
Day but no Stop Drinking Day

people who talk back to their TV sets

the fact that every moon in the solar
system has a cool name, except
Earth's

cliques you can't join

people who say "Life's tough; deal
with it"

family entertainment (theme parks,
movies, etc.) that families can no
longer afford

entertaining the macabre thought that, someday, worms will be eating you

being distracted by those weird flecks that float around inside your eye-balls

a growing but unprovable suspicion that the waiter has spit in your food

discovering that expensive tropical fish never survive outside of the Tropics

breaking all your New Year's resolutions by January 2nd

having to be shaved before surgery

any further news coverage of Joey
　　Buttafuoco and Amy Fisher

any further coverage of yet another
　　scandal rocking Britain's Royal
　　Family

realizing that the fatty, cholesterol-
　　laden skin is the only *really* tasty
　　part of a chicken

smarmy people

guys named Ned

when you ask a long-winded person
what time it is and they tell you
how to build a watch

all eight verses of the "On Top of
Spaghetti" song

why UFOs would abduct the uninter-
esting specimens who claim they
were taken onboard

when the car ahead blinks left for 20
miles before turning

when relatives mail you newspaper
   clippings, but you can't figure out
   why

never using a word like "harassment"
   because you're unsure of its pro-
   nunciation

when your job gets sent to Mexico

chihuahuas

wet blankets

dour Senator Dole

mall-rat kids

people who hang around celebrities
in order to bask in reflected lime-
light

yawners in your audience

nearly asphyxiating yourself trying a
hiccup cure

ingrates who never repay you for gifts
    or favors

people who give only because they
    expect to get something in return

when a suspicious-looking car parks
    in front of your house

people who remark that your child
    doesn't look like either of you

Bugs Bunny and Daffy Duck cartoons
    with all the "violence" cut out

being a risk-avoider in a relationship
    with a thrill-seeker

poems that don't rhyme

when your dog is a furry, four-legged
    pervert

every time interest rates take a dip
    after your loan rate has been
    locked in

catheters

highway repair work done during rush hours instead of late at night

Playboy readers who claim they buy it for the insightful articles

getting cramps when you're stranded in traffic

when you notice green fur on your sandwich in mid-bite

when all your appliances' plugs have three prongs, but your electric outlets have only two holes

having to hack off the third prong
     from electrical cords

people who can say "I love you" with
     belches

being layed off or otherwise unem-
     ployed

colorized movies

products that claim to help you lose
     weight while you sleep

when the dial on your TV breaks, and you have to use a pair of pliers to change channels

pillow tags that say "Do Not Remove Under Penalty of Law"

the hundreds of excuses family members have for avoiding housework

cleaning the crud off the floor under the refrigerator

when the grout of your bathroom tiles turns pink and pasty

when the appetizer and the main
course are served together

used cars advertised as "previously
owned"

scraping off the bumper stickers on
your new used car

the brilliant idea to install ATMs in
police stations to deter thefts

an anniversary present from your in-
laws so ugly you'll turn to stone if
you look directly at it

when a spring pops out of your shabby
couch as your guest sits down

people who try to convince you there's
a difference between a couch and
a sofa

motorists who plumb the depths of
their noses while driving

upstairs neighbors who vacuum at
6 A.M. on weekends

when your mom tells you to put on a
sweater because she's freezing

people who think topless bars are
high-class establishments

when the bar runs out of Beer Nuts

sold out shows at Vegas

having a powerful telescope, but ugly
neighbors

dinner guests who steal your silver-
ware

headless beer

guests who give you a hard time
    when you serve red wine with
    fish

guests who peek into your bathroom's
    medicine cabinet

signs on people's office doors pro-
    claiming who they are

that you can flunk a drug test from
    eating a poppy-seed bagel

when a twist-off cap spins round and
round and won't come off

going to the movies alone

awards for perfect attendance

when you wish upon a star and it
turns out to be an airplane

the smell of hospitals

inhospitable doctors

ruler scars from parochial school

the peppy people on early-morning
   exercise shows

living in a town with a dull-sounding
   name, like Plainview

living in a town whose name pro-
   vokes snickers, like Flushing

cigar smoke

soapdish gunk

when your car gets recalled

catching a 90-mph fastball with your
    bare hands

neighbors who never speak to you

the faint of heart

evildoers who get off with a slap on
the wrists

getting woozy and nauseated from
the gasoline fumes when filling
your tank

stepping on sharp pine needles in your
carpet for months after Christmas

Jerry Lewis's plans to remake *The
Nutty Professor*

the inventor of Twinkies who ate two
  everyday and lived to be eighty-
  five

the Lucky Charms leprechaun

proving empirically that is *is* possible
  to get pregnant the first time

cereal containing dehydrated fruit

an unsolved Rubik's Cube sitting on
  a shelf, silently mocking you

people who pick the raisins out of
   muffins, cereal, etc.

stool pigeons

pigeons—period

the fact that nearly half of all Ameri-
   cans never read a book

trivia buffs who spout little-known
   facts

---

people who step on ants deliberately

"Rush in '96" bumper stickers

when the window crank of your car
    snaps off

when an injured snarling raccoon
    takes refuge in your garage

claims of nonviolence by the propo-
    nents of the martial arts

oompah band music for more than
  five minutes

steel-drum music for more than two
  minutes

bagpipe music for more than two
  seconds

body mutilation in the name of art

uncultured people

when the clock in the stomach of your
statue of "Venus" stops running

your wedding pictures after the
divorce

rank amateurs

the corporate downsizing mania

products touted as "Incredible"

drivers who use radar detectors

that cute babies seem to grow up to
become ugly adults, and vice-versa

the fact that beauties are paid more
than beasts

when identical twins are always
dressed the same

elevator riders who won't step aside
to let you out

knee-jerk reactions

game hunters who insist they need
   assault weapons

bellboys with B.A.'s

when a videotape of a crime is insuf-
   ficient evidence

rumors and innuendo

deadbeat parents

bone-pulverizing handshakes

when no car will make the first move
    at a four-way stop

when the cop writing your ticket is
    younger than you

disliked nicknames that stick

getting stuck upside-down on a roller
coaster

"Beware of Attack Cat" signs

concert halls with tinny acoustics

eyestraining 3-D movies

when kids consider sports stars their
heroes

northeastern winters

people who jam Vermont every fall to
see the trees change colors

hitting every red light when you're
late

people with easy jobs, like weather
forecasters in Los Angeles

people who don't board planes by
row number

when the electric company says they
        must raise rates because customers
        didn't use enough electricity

when it smells like something died in
        your bathroom

defective disappearing ink

chronic complainers

movie critics who have never made a
        film

lose-lose scenarios

stretch marks

pet psychologists

paintings of weepy big-eyed kids sold
in shopping malls

that it's called *men*opause when only
women go through it

snooty luxury-car salespeople

those who talk the talk but don't walk
the walk

being unemployed on Labor Day

headcheese sandwiches

shredding your fingertips before realizing the bottle cap doesn't twist

wondering, if *Star Trek*'s technology is
so advanced, why Picard is bald

made-for-TV movies about the dis-
ease, murder, or teenage Lolita of
the week

pet owners who treat their animals
like children

the wimpy drivers who steer their cars
around parking lot speed bumps

how it never rains when you remem-
ber to take your umbrella

when your childhood memories start
   fading, or become clearer

when the kid in the upper bunk of
   your bunkbed is a bedwetter

people who flock to see the miracu-
   lous faces in unwashed windows

the speed with which the Christmas
   spirit packs up and leaves town

how by the time you get used to
   writing the correct year on checks,
   the year ends

when your ears burn after coming in
    from the cold

when you sneeze every time you go
    out into the sunlight

faster-than-a-speeding-bullet cham-
    pagne-bottle corks

Linda McCartney's singing

Milky Way "lite" candy bars

gizmos for shaving your sweaters

moving a piano up four flights of stairs

religious proselytizers who ring
   your doorbell early on Saturday
   mornings

school kids who throw their old
   sneakers over the telephone wires
   in front of your home

films about death or dying

movies based on *Saturday Night Live* skits

love affairs that died faster than Chevy
    Chase's talkshow

Lake Wobegon stories

the way all elevator riders mutely
    stare at the floor numbers

people who use the "sniff test" to de-
    cide what to wear

as you leave the plane, flight attendants who say "Bye-bye now"

the fact that only your nose keeps growing all your life

ham on Thanksgiving

when you have to eat at the kids' table

when your part in the school play was always a Tree

kids who refuse to dissect frogs in
biology classes .

geeks who use mechanical pencils

having to learn a dead language, like
Latin

when tall women are always described
as statuesque

news stories that mention women's
hair color, but not men's

grotesquely muscled weight lifters of
either gender

lighting the wrong end of a filtered
cigarette

food with zero fat, zero cholesterol,
and zero taste

rice cakes

last-minute Christmas shoppers

receiving sexy lingerie from very casual acquaintances

the fact that belly buttons are forbidden in the Sunday comics

that nobody seems to mind Donald Duck walking around bottomless

when TV shows recycle parts of old episodes to make a "new" episode

thirty-five-year-olds who still live at home

nouvelle cuisine's skimpy portions and
   outrageous prices

burnt pancakes

lazy cooks who buy pre-mashed
   potatoes and canned spaghetti

parsnips and Brussels sprouts

sticky kitchen floors

couples who sleep "spooned"

the thought that Ross Perot is rich
    enough to get himself cloned

being asked hard questions when
    you're sleepy

people who bite their toenails

unions

the Terrible Twos

when the kids pop corn without a lid
    on the pot

coming home to an empty apartment

bosses from Hell

dorky school uniforms

hammy actors

cold, clammy mornings

hotel rooms near a noisy elevator

people who know enough about something to be dangerous

having to get your ring cut off

promise renegers

deleted expletives

apocryphal stories, like the one about
the poodle being dried in a microwave

a car with one headlight beam that
shoots up at a bizarre angle

getting the bejesus scared out of you

living under powerlines

people with lots of knowledge but no
    imagination

the blatant spousal-abuse in the comic
    strip "Andy Capp"

whirling and spinning rides at amuse-
    ment parks that make you sick or
    brain-damaged

useless pockets on pajamas

people who give you conniptions

shushers in libraries

cult leaders

people who ask "How are you?" but
who couldn't care less

being at the end of a long check-out
line when buying ice cream

rotary telephones

clocks without numbers

calling sleazy bars lounges

standing in the unemployment line

pets who don't greet you at the door
    unless it's feeding time

clubs with secret initiation ceremonies

missing your afternoon nap

Hoosiers

Barry Manilow songs

MTV videos of rappers shouting
menacingly at you

people who know how to push your
     buttons

never finding your niche

free-floating anxiety

panic attacks

wasting hours watching blobs floating
     in a lava lamp

living next to a tennis court, being
   slowly driven mad by the "pongs"

discovering "secret sauce" is only
   ketchup and mayonnaise

getting goosed in a foreign city

that scientists can send people to the
   moon, but can't make pantyhose
   that won't run or snag

Ziggy comics

supermarket shoppers who take meat, decide they don't want it, and then leave it in another section

trying to fish the last pickle out of a jar

pudding that could double as brick mortar

discovering someone has written "Wash Me" on the back of your dirty car

when intelligence gets overwhelmed by hormones

people who still wear musk cologne

when booms go bust

those annoying TV station logos in
the lower-right-hand corner of
the screen

movie credits that show the date it was
made in roman numerals

people who respond to your expla-
nations with a "Yeah, whatever"

fatal flaws

type-A personalities

calendars featuring pictures of cats
dressed and posed like people

the casting for the movie *Interview With
a Vampire*

"We'll be right back after these mes-
sages"

silent letters in words, like the "g" in
    gnat

purchasing a videotape and never
    watching it more than once

getting cut out of a will

cars that hog two parking spaces

de-wedging a wedgie in public

when someone finishes your sentence for you

PA-system announcers who tap and blow into the microphone to see if it's on

sneakers squeaking on basketball courts

when you stop wondering what you're going to be, and realize this is it

laundromat patrons who dump your still-wet clothes on the floor so they can use the washer

when ocean-front houses get washed
    away by storms

forgetting how to use a slide rule

being the first one out in a game of
    musical chairs

the greasy film you can never wash
    off plastic food containers

people who give cute names to their
    body's appendages

Pat Buchanan

Spam recipes

the return of health-be-damned fast
food

the day the price of comic books went
from ten cents to twelve cents

clichéd sayings

jazz horn–players who sound like they're strangling a duck

hairy anchovies

that no one sends singing telegrams anymore

anything that promises to work "like a charm"

being told a standard lie, like the check's in the mail

people who hang out in coffeehouses, trying to act cool

carolers making a racket outside when you're trying to sleep

the neighbor's stereo blaring Gregorian chants

when there's a small crack in the window of your ant farm

having to stay over a weekend to get a cheaper air fare

lots of idle chatter about the weather

days when you don't speak to anyone

constellations that don't look anything
like what they're named after

Halley's Comet's last dismal "ap-
pearance"

when food servers pretend not to notice your gestures to get their
attention

when a lone restaurant diner occupies
a table for six

being shown the proper way to eat
artichokes after you've gulped
down a dozen leaves

product prices that end in "99 cents"
to make you think you're paying
less

when the scoop of ice cream topples
from your cone

an apartment window facing a brick
wall

pencil sharpeners that break off the point

mysteries with too many plot twists

sports figures who sell their autographs

people who smell like they bathed in cologne

seemingly healthy people who have handicapped-parking permits for their cars

getting cold spasms no matter how
slowly you wade into a chilly pool

Barbie dolls with better wardrobes
than you

Ken dolls with earrings

the insipid TV-viewing habits of the
"Nielsen Families"

TV commercials shot in a shaky,
hand-held camera style

poets who romanticize madness

e. e. cummings's use of lowercase let-
     ters in his poems

living a life of quiet desperation

lily gilders

hustlers who "clean" your windshield
     with a greasy rag and demand
     payment

the death of Frank Zappa

people who keep telling you how
    honest (talented, etc.) they are

leaving your lunch bag on a subway
    train

high-tech TV weather reports that you
    could duplicate by looking out a
    window

virtual reality's enormous potential to
    exacerbate loneliness

couples who have loud disputes in
   public

finding a piece of shell, not a pearl,
   in your oyster

that the silly rabbit never gets to eat
   the Trix

fungal growths on your lawn

flyers and ads for thigh-reducing cream

when your dog has to stop at every
bush and tree on the block

discovering that the interior of your
pot pie is hotter than molten lava

cops in doughnut shops

people who play records backwards

subway conductors who make cute an-
nouncements over the intercom

people who view all controversies only
in terms of black and white

when *It's a Wonderful Life* is on every
channel during the holidays

that we can put a computer on a chip,
but still can't put metal in the
microwave

how everyone who claims to have
lived a previous life was always a
king or queen, never a peasant
or serf

screechy exotic birds that bite

gray hair on places other than your
head

when younger people make more
money than you

seeing millions of people not at work
in the middle of the afternoon

expiration dates on containers of sour
cream

pouring curdled milk into your coffee

that "faux" has replaced the word "phony"

friends who always shoot down your ideas

smarmy morning DJ teams

flashbacks of Park's Sausages commercials (*"More* Park's Sausages, Mah, please!!")

drivers who get belligerent when you signal them to turn on their lights making the same mistake twice

when all you've done has been for
naught

when another kid sneezes on your kid

candy machines that eat your spare
change

when your kids spell out naughty
words with their Alpha-Bits

walking down an icy hill

why nobody can recognize Clark Kent
just because he removes his glasses

trying to make a graceful recovery
after falling at a skating rink

the "mazes" deliberately built into de-
partment stores' floor plans

becoming a slave to routine

when the car ahead turns on its windshield washer and the water hits
your car

coworkers who remind you every
Wednesday that it's "Hump Day"

foods described as savory

MBAs in BMWs

unsolved disappearances, like Amelia
Earhart's, Judge Crater's, and
Jimmy Hoffa's

interminable meetings

people who can sleep with their eyes
    open

sloppy drunks

neat drunks

trying to thread a needle with a very
    limp thread

being diabetic and living in Hershey,
   Pennsylvania

being German and having to watch
   Hogan's Heroes

having ears that stick out

settling down too young

babysitters who eat everything in
   your fridge

talking to someone who doesn't make
   eye contact

when people your age start discussing
   their medical problems

Mr. Blackwell's "Worst Dressed" list

sitting in a Naugahyde chair on a
   sticky summer day

a slow golfing party ahead of yours

coy phrases for going to the bathroom
(e.g.: going to see a man about a
horse; to powder my nose; to the
little girls' room, etc.)

biting hard on a prune you thought
was pitted

prune-flavored ice cream

long-distance callers who forget about
the difference in time zones

when your bottle of correction fluid
coagulates into a thick paste

when the paper cutter makes ragged
   edges

"Jingle Bells" sung by barking dogs

TV interference from your neighbor's
   CB radio

people who wear a chip on their
   shoulder

people who stand around in book-
   stores, reading but not buying the
   books

people who can't take a hint

lifetime smokers who want to sue the
tobacco companies when they
become ill

aftershave that smells like old gym
socks

products spelled with a kitschy "k"
(e.g.: Krazy Glue, Kandy Korn)

getting caught singing along with the
Muzak when taken off "hold"

people who *tell you* when you ask "How are you?"

when you sit on a chair and it breaks

people with children, grandchildren, cats, dogs, etc., and a wallet full of pictures

arriving at a party overdressed

when you attend the theater and the star has been replaced by the understudy

twin beds on a honeymoon

people who fill out their withdrawal
    slips at the teller's window

when approaching a pair of doors,
    always pushing the locked door

spouses who insist that underwear be
    ironed

when your favorite snow-globe springs
    a leak

when the phone company changes
your area code

moving and changing your mailing
address

dubious weather folklore, like "it will
rain if cows lie down in the pas-
ture"

trying to suppress a sneeze when you
have diarrhea

potbellied pigs as pets

people who opt for liposuction instead of dieting

neighbors who park two or three junked cars in their front yards

when your biological clock begins winding down

advertising jingles from your childhood that pop into your brain and keep you awake

being unable to remove a screw because your screwdriver mangled it

when fish you'd never eat is disguised
    with an exotic new name (e.g.:
    monkfish renamed orange roughy)

elaborate car alarms on junky cars

when someone admonishes you to
    "chill"

sentences that begin "When I was a
    kid . . ."

that no nickel is refunded when you
    put a quarter in a twenty-cent pay
    phone

kids wearing ultra-baggy pants

the fact that you have to work until May 10th just to pay taxes

stairwells that smell like ammonia

Charlie Chaplin in ads for IBM computers

service with a scowl

when everyone in a boat is rowing in
different directions

books that take 500 pages to tell a
simple story

loud obnoxious background music
while you're dining

loud obnoxious people in the background while you're dining

when the dealer takes too long to
shuffle the cards

sitting in front of a bugle-blower at
the ball park

art exhibitions by mass murderers

Amway salespeople

when someone gives your kid a toy
gun

people who still play Trivial Pursuit

gagging on a too-large oyster

advice columnists

parents who force kids to take tap-dancing lessons

people who claim to have valid psychological reasons for being such jerks

trying to find the one dead bulb that knocks out the whole string of Christmas lights

people who ask "So what's your point?"

when you reach the age when passing
    gas no longer amuses anyone

being a dinner guest in a home where
    they let the dog lick the plates
    clean

looters

wine snobs

etiquette teachers

a bloody-stool false alarm, brought
    about by eating beets

five final exams in one week

sitting in the bus seat directly over
    one of the rear wheels

when a nail bends over while you're
    hammering

whoever first decided that TV weather forecasters should act goofy

people who play little tunes on their pushbutton phones

being beaten by the odds

using less and less toilet paper as you near the end of the roll

the crowd of people appearing at the counter when you purchase laxatives trying to peel an over-ripe avocado

that you can't buy a moon-rock ring

belly-flopping when attempting a
graceful dive

eating after brushing your teeth

when your father puts a compass on
the car's dashboard

the Tilt-A-Whirl ride at fairs

corny state mottoes, like "Live Free
   or Die"

Alaska having no state nickname

cars with "ah-oo-gah" horns

only fourteen minutes of fame

cities that are famous for odd things,
like beer or artichokes

varicose veins

people who get bent out of shape
when a baby is breast-fed in
public

imitation crabmeat

wishy-washy people

no-refund policies

people whose idea of roughing it is
watching a black-and-white TV

that no kid will ever again be named
Adolf

limited warranties

the baby boomers' influence on culture

a mood-altering bug

the power of placebos

Las Vegas touting itself as a family-
    fun spot

people who ask "What's your prob-
    lem?"

voice mail

errant ballbearings on wood floors

ice shoved down your shorts

extremely defensive people

when some joker interleaves the pages
of two books together

people with bulging eyes and narrow
pupils

when your best friend becomes too
    predictable

dislocating your shoulder

trick knees

having the kibosh put on your plans

compasses with no sense of direction

that kids don't know how to play
    marbles anymore

seeing the present you gave someone
    in the garbage

undated correspondence

when people speak a foreign language
    only when you're in the room

mobs at the mall

Barbara Walters's lisp

when spaghetti sticks to the bottom of
the pot

people who wear black socks with
shorts

getting grossed out from seeing the
JFK assassination footage

when the wind sends your empty trash
cans barreling down the street

beautiful Julia Roberts marrying geeky
   Lyle Lovett

vitamin-enriched sugary cereals

leaky implants

French poodles

painting yourself into a corner

Murphy's Law

syrupy pianists in hotel lounges

backseat drivers

that there are no Good Humor ice
cream trucks anymore

impulse purchases that you later regret

discovering a tattoo after you sober
    up

home brewery kits

Salad Shooters

tofu ice cream

when your best friend moves far away

when your PC's hard disk crashes

the Dan Quayle Museum

variant spellings, such as "lite" for
    "light," "thru" for "through," etc.

pie eaters who assuage their guilt by
    putting Sweet 'n Low in their
    coffee

people who can watch slasher flicks,
    but cringe at the sight of a hypo-
    dermic needle

sensory overload

victimization

bad choices

unsynchronized clocks

that everybody wants to go to Heaven,
    but no one wants to die

people who must be right, always

when Mom sends you to the store to buy embarrassing personal products for her

when the exterminator covers your house with a circus tent the size of Montana

when your Silly Putty oozes into the carpet

readers who lick their fingertips to turn pages

babies switched at birth

people who carry dozens of pens in
    their shirt pockets

when your name winds up on a
    mailing list for kinky "novelties"

receiving a rejection from the college
    of your choice

classmates who wear their varsity-
    letter sweaters everywhere

people who call the movies "cinema"

that there are no more Tom Carvel
    commercials

when you think of the perfect come-
    back hours after the argument
    ends

a mutt barking when you're trying to
    think

discovering there's a spoon down the
    garbage disposal after turning it
    on

when the year goes by in a blur

people who think Joan of Arc was
    Noah's wife

people who still believe that pro-
    fessional wrestling is real

jackknifed trucks tying up traffic

tanning salons near the beach

death-bed laments

eating anything in aspic

sprouting hair where you don't want
    it, losing it where you do

that Iceland is green and Greenland
    is covered with ice

people who stuff and hang dead ani-
    mals' heads on their walls

body piercing below the chin

feeling alone even in a crowd

getting skin or hair caught in a zipper

not finding out about a great sale until
    it's over

not being able to wash your hair for
    a couple of days

the cancellation of Domino's thirty-
minute pizza delivery guarantee

half-baked ideas

homework over the holidays

Frank Sinatra singing "My Way"

when your kite gets caught in a tree

Monday-morning quarterbacks

people with 20/20 hindsight

retroactive income taxes

excessive home-video zooms that make
    you seasick

when your first name ends with
    "-Bob" or "-Boy" (e.g.: Joe-Bob,
    John-Boy)

when your car phone fades out

hangover cures that turn your stomach

self-aggrandizers

when people say "Get with the program"

having to think twice before honking at strangers

children's stories that have no point,
like "Jack and the Beanstalk"

when pants with tissues in the pockets
wind up in the wash

forks with hardened gunk between
the tines

when countries change names, making
all your maps and globes obsolete

when the only song you can play on
your guitar is "My Dog Has
Fleas"

smart-mouthed TV sitcom kids

when it's too smoggy to see a rain-
   bow

that there's no background sound-
   track in real life, like there is in
   movies

when a person wins the lottery but
   doesn't quit his or her job

pipe smokers who think it smells good

when diners pour ketchup on filet
  mignon

when you're young, withholdings for
  Social Security

car corrosion from road salt

suspecting that thirty years from now,
  red meat and cigarettes will be
  found to be good for you

that *Cheers* isn't on anymore

when the oil companies have you
over a barrel

Midwestern accents

an ancient bottle of chutney in the
back of your refrigerator

challenging a Scrabble® word, and
finding it in the dictionary

the thought that disco might make a
comeback

when they broadcast actual 911 emergency calls on TV

waking up with a stiff neck

pop psychology

radio shrinks

mile-wide, inch-deep philosophies

therapy junkies

velvet paintings of dogs playing poker

people who believe a yellow light
means speed up

when you rent too many movies for
one night's viewing

when stagecoach wheels appear to
spin backwards in movies

guests who use too much toilet paper
   in one sitting

yogurt with no fat but 300 calories

a hockey game without a bloody fight

your driver's license photo

friends who urge you to eat alligator
   meat, etc., by saying "It tastes just
   like chicken!"

dopes who take "smart drugs"

jinxes

hearing the occupant lock the doors
    when you walk past a parked car

having to traipse through a maze of
    ropes at the bank when you're
    the only person in line

people who wear their watches to
    bed

the queasy feeling you get when an elevator starts or stops too suddenly

when largish line dancers do the "tush-push"

discovering a drowned roach at the bottom of your cup of coffee

when the only song you can play on the piano is "Heart and Soul"

having your bluff called

receiving a gift CD when you don't
    own a player

when the plane's overhead compart-
    ment is full before you reach
    your seat

a cold toilet seat

a still-warm toilet seat

when valets park the expensive cars
    in front of the restaurant

people who drive flashy red sports
    cars

pink Rolls-Royces

trying to kick someone's butt on a
    computer bulletin board system

when the only time you see your rela-
    tives is at weddings and funerals

relatives who ask "So when are you
    going to have children?"

when you have a child, relatives who ask "So when are you going to have another?"

losing an argument

music that sounds like steel piano wires snapping

New Age music

receiving dozens of mail-order catalogs for stuff you'd never buy, like clothing for lumberjacks

the latest yuppy toy: Personal Digital
    Assistants

the idea that quality and quantity are
    mutually exclusive

"quality time"

loaded dice

fuzzy dice dangling from rearview
    mirrors

drivers who put dogs in the backs of
pickup trucks

squatting with spurs on

instruction books for living your life

that no one ever reads the instructions
until something goes wrong

feeling like a small cog in a very large
machine

when your car's engine knocks

falling for the old look-up-in-the-sky
gag

having to get up to go to the bathroom more than once a night

trying to navigate your way to the
bathroom at night without open-
ing your eyes

when the kids don't flush

people from other parts of the country who claim *you* have a funny accent

restaurants that automatically add a tip to your bill

telling a friend about the great job you applied for, and they end up getting it

the song "Memory" from *Cats*

five-second Walk lights

the pitiful Recommended Daily Allowance for vitamins

the plot by fruit farmers to get you to eat five servings of fruit a day

when your five-year-old starts using the f-word

creaky rocking chairs

buying your first pair of bifocals

buying your first car with wood siding

a fungal growth under your toenail

when rotund people wear suspenders

getting lost in a giant warehouse store

movies that intentionally try to jerk
your tears

people who get their thrills by humiliating you

being asked "What do you do?" the moment you meet someone

expecting to be blown up whenever you relight a pilot light

puncturing a water pipe when hammering a nail into your wall

trying to unscrew a broken lightbulb's base out of the socket calling 911 and being put on hold

waking up with a coated tongue

smart alecks with low IQs

gender-free snow people

would-be singers who couldn't carry a
   tune if it had handles on it

when parents say "You'd lose your
head if it wasn't screwed on"

acts of decapitation and disem-
bowelment in kids' video games

double-parkers

the one that got away

fans of criminals

being quoted out of context

that "almost" doesn't count

when someone with your last name
    commits a hideous crime, and it's
    reported on CNN

beehive hairdos

dwarf tossers

shopping mall security guards on power trips

TV ads for personal-injury attorneys that feature client testimonials

basketball players who shatter the glass backboards

when football fans dance shirtless in sub-zero weather

gamblers who play their cards close to the vest

audiences who go "wooh-wooh" in
lieu of applause

never using more than five percent of
what you studied in school

diagramming sentences

knowing you've forgotten more things
than you'd ever admit

people whose lips move when they
read

kids who wear T-shirts stretched to
their knees

paying big bucks for abstract art that
your three-year-old could have
drawn better

emotional blackmail

the scent that lingers on you after
wearing a leather jacket

spectators at fireworks displays who
say "ooh" and "ahh"

people who go on the Tunnel-of-Love
    ride by themselves

coffee grounds in your cup of espresso

parents who say "Because I say so"

people who want simplistic answers to
    everything

making mountains out of molehills

parents who blame society's ills on rock and roll, comic books, Beavis and Butt-head, etc.

losing a wager

being unceremoniously ejected from your job

when they changed Darrins on *Bewitched*

that Elvis's death was the shrewdest career move he ever made three-hour movies

when spicy hot food burns on the
    way down, and on the way out

telecommunications satellites in space
    that are being used to bring us
    Ren & Stimpy

people who hem and haw

when actors sell their Oscars

drunk guests who pee in the bushes
    at your party

the school-yard bully

police officers hiding with their radar
    guns

having to follow orders from an idiot

unquestioned authority

getting a lump of coal in your Christmas stocking

tropical fish that spend all their time hiding behind aquarium vegetation

phone pranksters

kids' party clowns

overstuffed napkin dispensers

the loss of the capacity for wonder

when your leaf collection includes poison ivy

replacing lights in a chandelier hanging over a stairwell

getting the polarities reversed when jump-starting a car

fraternity hazings

people who put the seat up but miss
the bowl

Hummel figurines

getting loaded on eggnog

going to Confession after a multi-year
lapse

Michael Jackson's ownership of most
of the Beatles' music

soap that sinks

when the liquor-store clerk recognizes
    your teenager

"Don't call us; we'll call you"

people who pinch all the pieces of
    boxed chocolates to see what's in
    them

the absence of toothpicks after eating
    corn-on-the-cob

doctors who smoke

ex-smokers who harass others about
    quitting

a former lover—now alive and kick-
    ing—who vowed "I'll die without
    you"

when people start saying "You look
    wonderful!" on your birthday

cantankerous old coots

the surfeit of stand-up comics

people who still won't eat meat on
    Friday

when a couple calls off their engage-
    ment after you've given them a
    gift

putting a worm on a hook

when someone discovers your mate's
    private pet name for you

people's fear of ghosts, when it's the
   living who are scarier

when a president gets a two-hundred-
   dollar haircut

when a billionaire gets a five-dollar
   haircut

people who grin all the time

feeling faintly ridiculous most of the
   time

contemplating the expanding universe, and your insignificance in the face of it

replying "I'm fine" when you're not

when hotels can't find your reservation, and they're full

receiving bills for $0.00 and a payment envelope

turning 21, 30, 40, 50, or 65

dollar-a-quart designer water

always wanting a chemistry set, never
  getting it

people who eat the cream filling in
  an Oreo before devouring the
  cookie

getting dizzy at the airport luggage
  carousel watching the bags go
  round

working the graveyard shift

people who want to be cremated, sprinkled into the sea, and end up as fish food

when greeting-card companies invent new holidays just to sell more cards (e.g.: Bosses' Day)

Olympic mascots

that synchronized swimming is an Olympic event

people who start billion-dollar businesses in their garages

not having a garage

cleaning the litterbox

souvenirs of a lousy relationship

not getting your record albums back
    after a break-up

the distortion of time on soap operas

meat loaf that could do double-duty
   as a doorstop

not being able to tell when pump-
   style toothpaste is nearly finished

the new paper money that looks like
   it's counterfeit

bullfighting

people who shouldn't wear tank tops,
   but do

people who bail out of events early in
order to beat the rush to the
parking lot

the Susan B. Anthony coin

when your grown-up children tell you
all the things you never knew
about

pencil-pushing bean counters

forgetting your wallet is on the roof
of your car as you drive off

painting your house every three years

when your desk drawer slides off the rails

being called "Mr." on the phone when you're a "Ms."

the ever-growing fee banks charge for bounced checks

being able to hear the high-pitched noise that TVs emit

when your partner answers the phone
    during an intimate moment

when your fake vomit loses its power
    to revolt

carrying the burden of unfulfilled
    potential

the last day of summer

the first day of winter

going to all the trouble of getting someone a gift that she already has

white flossing speckles on your bathroom mirror

bicyclists who wear fancy riding out-
fits

getting a nose ring after it becomes
passé

fanny packs worn over suits

the *Will Rogers' Follies*

sound bites

photo ops

that Fabio has a better chest than
    most men—and women, too

when your hearing's shot from years
    of live-music concerts

the obliviousness of Walkman wearers

compassion fatigue

discovering your engagement ring is
actually cubic zirconium

Shari Lewis looking exactly the same
as she did thirty years ago

anything "Jurassic"

people whose total knowledge of eco-
    nomics is the phrase "supply and
    demand"

disruptions to your routine

Elton John's "hair"

your agent's ten percent

TV shows about fishing for bass

Jack Frostbite nipping off your toes

people who fish for compliments

finding only microscopic bits of
    chicken in your Chinese Chicken
    Salad

bad puns involving fish (e.g.: "I did
    that on porpoise!")

all work and no play

that all the safe toys are boring

firecrackers with short fuses

never having a BB gun because "you'll
    put your eye out"

the perversity of nature

when your ficus tree drops its leaves

when someone who wears dark glasses
    is called visionary

diners who steal sugar packets from
    restaurants

sitting on a beaded carseat cover when
    you have hemorrhoids

dishes, pans, etc., that are too big to
    lay flat in your sink

moving a refrigerator and scarring
    the floor

when your cats whine for food whenever you run the electric can
opener

that cats have nine lives

not being able to afford to shop at
K Mart

when your pet jumps up on the bed,
interrupting an intimate moment

people who abandon their pets

being left-handed when all the desks
    are for righties

Marky Mark underwear ads

anatomically-correct dolls

having unrealistic expectations for
    yourself

when people say "Close, but no cigar"

perfectionists who don't realize how
imperfect that trait makes them

vending-machine cappuccino

watching drinkers and smokers com-
mit suicide in slow-motion

jumpers and other suicides who leave
a nasty mess to be cleaned up

when the crowd yells "Jump! Jump!"

Highlights for Children's "Goofus & Gallant"

the Romper Room "Do-Bee"

being taxed for schools when you're childless

getting soaked by a water balloon

people who get cable just to watch the Weather Channel

that more people wanted to see Heidi's list than *Schindler's List*

locks on the doors of twenty-four-hour convenience stores

people posing nude on the cover of *Rolling Stone*

"belated" greeting cards

receiving a belated birthday card from your twin

how CDs were supposed to be impervious to scratches and last forever

the years you didn't have color TV because your parents were waiting for it to be perfected

owning an old color TV on which people always look green

shoppers who block the aisles in supermarkets

when a Macy's Thanksgiving Day Parade balloon is snagged by a lamppost when people see the Rose Bowl Parade on TV and decide to move to California

mail from the IRS stamped "Official Business"

kissy-kissy aunts who closely resemble lamprey eels

needing to be a rocket scientist to do your own taxes

people who have a "system" for playing the horses

people who throw darts at newspapers and make a fortune in the
stock market

infrequent phone callers who expect
you to recognize them by voice

trendy new "clear" products (e.g.: clear
beer)

"new and improved" products

when small items, like diamonds, fall
and disappear into your shag
carpet

when your barber makes better economic forecasts than the experts

flashers and other pervs

words overused into meaninglessness, such as "codependent," "dysfunctional," etc.

when your shrink discusses your problems with other patients

when "customer satisfaction guaranteed" translates into "when it breaks (and it will), we'll grudgingly try to fix it"

a bad case of the stomach flu

getting an expensive medical test and
finding nothing's wrong

going to an emergency room for a
heart attack that turns out to be
gas

fuzzy covers on toilet tanks that pre-
vent the seat from staying up

when dead actors are resurrected
electronically and forced to appear in cola commercials

wiseguys in banks who ask "Any free
   samples?"

wildly inaccurate five-day weather
   forecasts

wind-chill factors in the minus terri-
   tory

extremely cold air that freezes your
   eyelids shut and makes your
   nostrils sting

frozen water pipes bursting

people whose latest status symbol is an Internet address

calling pyramid schemes multi-level marketing

people who can't find the working end of a hammer

when people ask "Does it hurt?" after you hammer your thumb

working as a temp

mothers and daughters discussing hygiene products in TV ads

people who say "ax," as in "Can I ax you something?"

the dearth of hit songs that spotlight the saxophone

kids who go surfing before sunrise

when your cup of hot coffee slides off the dashboard

jelly doughnuts without any jelly

eating a powdered doughnut while
wearing a dark suit

language lessons that promise you'll
speak like a native in two weeks

the "dispensable crew member" who
always gets killed on *Star Trek*
episodes

chunky wristwatches

people who never blink

having to look up the spelling of
    "rhythm" every time you use it

media hype

shaving with a rusty razor

motorists who shave, apply makeup,
    etc., at red lights

people who can't walk and chew gum
at the same time

people who do too many things at
the same time

dates with "octopus arms"

eating shredded wheat when you
have a sore throat

when your kid asks "Guess what I
just got tattooed?"

Mighty Morphin Power Rangers

motel TVs with cigarette burns in the
    cabinet

philosophy majors

having a mind that wanders

hiking for hours only to come back to
    where you began

when you're doing 55, and all the cars are passing you

eating up your lunch hour by waiting in a line

disgusting descriptive phrases like "a pitcher of warm spit"

when eating a ham sandwich, wondering what part of the pig you're chewing

talking to somebody with coffee on their breath

family feuds

the stupid ending to *Romeo and Juliet*

grunge fashion and other oxymorons

Michael Keaton as Batman

screen doors wrecked by climbing kitties

playing second fiddle

when your guacamole dip turns a
    putrid shade of brown

bendable potato chips

drooling uncontrollably after receiving
    a shot of novocaine

when your plane is delayed, even
    though you got to the airport two
    hours early

vapid in-flight airplane music

phony sound effects in Kung-Fu
    movies

when servers take your plate away
    prematurely

dates who order the most expensive
    meal on the menu

breaking one plate in a set of eight

earsplitting PA-system feedback

slipping an uncapped marker pen into your shirt pocket

drivers who empty their ashtrays in parking lots

when you overhear a loudmouth explaining something and you know he's wrong

bomb scares

lost drivers who refuse to stop to ask
for directions

salespeople who say "I'll be right with
you" and then go to lunch

ketchup-bottle cap crud

sappy daily affirmations

people who aren't sure if Moby Dick
is the whale or the man

when the self-cleaning oven has to be scrubbed

suffering killer heartburn after eating a knish

"I may be slow, but I'm ahead of you" bumper stickers

people who peep under public restroom stall doors

receiving a dozen phone books each year that you never use

Catch 22's, like needing experience to get a job, but first needing a job to get the experience required

making an embarrassing Freudian slip in front of your shrink

shaking your proctologist's hand

dicing your fingernail when chopping onions

talking car alarms that say "Move *away* from the vehicle!"

reading everything you never wanted to know about Howard Stern's love life

discovering that your private cordless phone conversations can be eavesdropped on by anyone with a short-wave radio

how wall-hanging TV screens are always "just ten years away"

errant shopping carts careening around the parking lot

dents in your car from errant shopping carts

sharp-clawed cats that like to knead
soft parts of your body

the fuzz on kiwifruit

cars that play chicken with trains

buying Dante's *Divine Comedy* because
you thought it was a humor book

three-minute red lights; ten-second
green lights

gamblers who hit the jackpot with
their *last* coin

admitting your mistake and then realizing no one knew you made one

losing weight after you buy a new suit

unwittingly rubbing black ink from a
freshly printed newspaper onto
your nose

talkative people who need to clear
their throats and don't

automated phone pitches that ask you
to stay on the line

dumping a friend's call to answer a
sales pitch

wearing ankle-high boots in calf-high
snow

having wine spilled on you at the beginning of a party

fortune cookies containing proverbs,
not fortunes

when the person who collects all the
    money from your lunch party
    doesn't leave a tip

spilling soda into the computer key-
    board

twisted-up phone cords

being a "Junior"

that almost everywhere you go, every
    place looks the same

that this second took eons to get
    here, and now will never exist
    again

waiting ten minutes for service before
    realizing you have to take a
    number

that overused "morphing" special
    effect

doing the same old thing every day

going through too many changes at
    once

people who quote Bob Dylan lyrics

when it costs more to repair your VCR than to buy a new one

when your favorite little restaurant gets discovered

being unable to change reality with a click of the remote

when the odds for success are 98%, and you're in the 2% group

being unable to stifle your laughter at
    a twisted joke

forgetting to rinse out your thermos
    bottle, then opening it next year

getting sacked

three-legged sack races

people who grunt to acknowledge
    what you're saying

stories that use an evil twin as a plot device

people who go to a French restaurant and order a burger

buying a cheap, hard mattress and regretting it nightly

receiving fondue sets as wedding gifts

when any part of your body gets chafed

when the value of your home drops
    thirty grand in a year

that medical science can't perform IQ
    implants

hitting the "runner's wall"

kids who win spelling bees

slipped discs

when debtors skip town

passing a test by the skin of your teeth

people who photocopy their body parts

M&M's that melt in your hand, not in your mouth

when toddlers won't eat anything you cook unless it's smothered in ketchup

trying to get the "How Am I Driving?" number from a truck doing 90 mph

doing a wheelie and falling off your bike

the billions of people who claim to have been at Woodstock

that the hardest work is thinking

being unable to think of an easier way to make a living

people who you can trust only as far
as you can throw them

that the person who loves the least
controls the relationship

Campbell's doofy new slogan: "Never
Underestimate the Power of
Soup"

discovering what tripe is after you've
eaten a bowlful

the retort "In your dreams"

when somebody calls you "Pal"

finding a pink slip in your pay envelope

never finding gloves in a glove compartment

stores that don't open until 10 A.M.

goody-goodies

cold sores

products that have existed for years but no one wants, like video telephones

atheists who say "Bless you" when you sneeze

dogs that howl horribly at the sound of a passing siren

living near both a basset hound and a hospital

antisocial people who won't buy an
answering machine

ads promising to beat any competitor's
price—but only if *you* do the ex-
tensive research required to find
that lower price

uncles who shake your hand with a
joy buzzer

being awakened at daybreak by a
neighbor's crowing rooster

when farmers are paid not to grow
stuff

when a juvenile delinquent snaps the
antenna off your car

toy cellular phones

having a name that everyone makes
the same lame joke about

having to sit next to the hot radi-
ators throughout school because of
alphabetical seating plans

lackeys and flunkies

when your mobile crashes down
   around your ears

all the hoopla over the coming 500-
   channel info highway, when it's
   only TV

inhaling a fly

spandex bodysuits

the smell of Band-Aids

kids who pluck the wings off butter-
flies

taking shorthand notes in class that
you can't decipher later

when you don't hear the restaurant
page for your party

bubble gum cards about serial killers

being unable to taste any difference
between premium popcorn and
the cheap stuff

having to eat crow

continuing debates over battles fought
    long ago

committees

when the back of your dress gets
    tucked into your pantyhose after
    you use the restroom

blowhards

when people hock up phlegm while
    you're eating

a man in a women's aerobics class

being spat on—or worse—by a zoo
    animal

when your kids see the elephants
    mating at the zoo and ask a ton
    of questions

kissing someone wearing dental braces

when servers introduce themselves to
customers

when customers introduce themselves
to servers

those who leave a tip even when the
service was lousy

birds that squawk loudly in the middle
of the night

the scratchy condition of library
phonograph records

mind-game players

overlooking allowable tax deductions

low lifes

narcissists

people who can fake sincerity

having to use the word "alleged"

trying to please everybody

washboard-flat bellies

when the film developer makes his
own set of your swimsuit pictures

spending eternity in a doctor's waiting
room

California's undeserved reputation for
flakiness

carpoolers who honk when picking someone up at 5 A.M.

when high-wire circus acts use a safety net

Katie Couric's perkiness

people who would rescue a drowning pet before a drowning stranger

cooking live lobsters

having to wear a lobster bib

getting busted for running a light at a
completely deserted intersection

losing precious sleep over a crossword
puzzle

when people wear golfing clothes to
any place other than a golf course

garage-sale sponsors who never take
their signs down

confidants who don't keep your se-
crets

spraining your neck at a planetarium

New Englanders who call water
   fountains bubblers and hero
   sandwiches grinders

having to get up to turn over your
   laser disc

picking up litter with a poker and
   stabbing your foot

selling your home in a recession

giving your pet a pill

the gruesome endings of most classic
fairy tales

when your kid can't sleep after hearing
a scary fairy tale

when the "You Are Here" spot is
missing on mall maps

bowl haircuts

button-fly jeans when you've got the
    runs

getting on the wrong line at the DMV

the loose strand in each forkful of
    spaghetti that hits your chin

servers who insist on reeling off long
    memorized menus when you al-
    ready know what you want

when your lobster is missing a claw

sky-high airport food prices

books or movies alleged to be "wacky"

overrated regional cuisine, like New
York pizza, Chicago ribs, Texas
BBQ, and LA tacos

when your mate's idea of fancy
cooking is stirring onion soup
mix into sour cream

bad cooks who could burn water

no desserts in Japanese restaurants

the statistic that you'll spend six
months of your life at traffic lights

that your new car depreciates the
moment you drive it off the
dealer's lot

unlockable Ziploc bags

ornery people

when a bank's ATM is friendlier than
    its human tellers

the empty sections of bun on either
    end of a wiener

air you can see

smog you can taste

itchy pajamas

purses that seem to contain a black
    hole

driving past a car on fire

graffiti etched into windows

preppy names, like Muffy and Boots

a coffee table made of an industrial
    cable spool

revisiting your childhood home and
    discovering it's not as big as you
    remember

when the salad bar is out of your
favorite dressing

restaurants that have all the decora-
tive books and knickknacks glued
down

the present you spent twenty minutes
wrapping that gets ripped open
in five seconds

when your baby spits up on you right
after you've dressed

ads that use the phrase "most unique"

straining your brain trying to grasp
the twists of logic inherent in
time travel

a window-shopping driver ahead of
you

when your poinsettia dies a week
before Christmas

searching for your sunglasses when
they're on top of your head

door-to-door salespeople

too many soft drink choices (e.g.: diet,
   no caffeine, original formula, etc.)

coming to the inescapable conclusion
   that dieting makes you fat

things that implode

the wretched job market

the myth of lifetime employment

when your job's no fun anymore

dining by yourself

meat-market singles' bars

country-music songs about guys who
raise hell, drink, cheat, and then
wonder why their baby left 'em

a plot hole big enough to drive a
bulldozer through

Colonel Sanders still "hawking" fried
chicken many years after his death

pigeons perched on a windowsill that
watch while you eat

when birds come up to your car in
the fast-food parking lot and beg
for scraps

ventriloquist acts on the radio

lampshade-wearing guests who fancy
themselves the life of your party

when "of" is shortened to just "o" (e.g.:
barrel o' laffs, bowl o' cherries,
etc.)

soap-on-a-rope as an anniversary present

spinoffs of low-rated TV shows

the QVC home-shopping channel

Shannen Doherty, a.k.a. "Brenda"

Michael Jordan's retirement

jerks who parachute into boxing rings

competition instead of cooperation

the Biospherians

strangely named bands, like Smashing
   Pumpkins

offensively named bands, like Dead
   German Tourists

parents who give their kids Easter
   chicks, then later eat them

"Next Window" signs

choosing the wrong language at an English/Spanish ATM

discovering you've been mispronouncing a favorite phrase all your life, like "faux paux"

people who wear shorts in the dead of winter

physicians who get insulted if you don't call them "Doctor"

doctors who always call *you* by your
   first name

people who don't know what or
   where their uvula is

putting snow chains on your tires

day-old sushi

when a parking ticket blows off your
   windshield

people who call BMWs beemers

oil spots on your garage floor

parents who take seven-year-olds to
horror movies

when an asteroid has a half-million-
mile "near miss" with the Earth

secret radiation experiments per-
formed by our government

knowing that ketchup is half sugar

when voters act surprised to learn
    that politicians often break their
    campaign promises

sickos who make death threats at
    shopping mall Santas

slow fast food

customers who expect four-star food
    and service at fast-food joints

ascot wearers

sidewalk jewelry salespeople

buying suspect-quality meat products
from a sidewalk vendor

when you can see the string holding
up the *Enterprise*

kids in a hurry to grow up

adults who have forgotten what it was
like to be a kid

getting typecast

receiving a gift of cheese balls and
   miniature sausages

kissing a smoker

not hearing bells, or seeing fireworks,
   when you fall in love for real

appliances with too many bells and
   whistles

workaholics

chocoholics

off-color hotel TV sets

farting once in freshman gym class
and being called "Stinky" for the
next four years

when cartoon characters' lips aren't
in synch with the dialogue

that conscience doth not make cow-
ards of us all

deceptive movie previews that get you
to go see the turkey

Mazda Miata owners

Toyota trucks modified to read "Toy"

wondering if "a Toyota" was an in-
tentional palindrome

cars that cut through the corner gas
station to make a turn

reserved parking spaces for the company's bigshots

being behind an indecisive family of eight in the drive-through line

that Andy Rooney gets paid for what he does

owning an old video game system that they stopped making cartridges for

when people want to fix things that ain't broken

buggy software

being unable to tell a kilobyte from a
   trilobite

when TV shows are "dumbed down"
   to increase the ratings

people who think that the smell of
   mouthwash is better than onions

eating milk and pickles at the same
   meal

when the person sitting next to you
on the plane tells crash stories

that credit-card interest is no longer
tax deductible

taking mega-doses of vitamins that
just end up enriching the sewer
system

moving back home with your parents

crime reenactment shows on TV that
wackos use as training films

believing the line "There will always
be another time"

seeing dead people's most personal
private possessions on display in
flea markets

the feel of your feet lifting off the floor
of a plummeting roller coaster

Dick Clark beginning to show signs
of aging

conjugal visits for prison inmates

getting locked out of the housing
market

trimming your fingernail just a little
too close

neighbors who never take down their
Christmas lights

condo association members

taxpayers who wait till April 14th to
start their returns

holiday blahs and the summertime
blues

suffering in silence

falling off your rocker

when your brain buzzes from too
many cups of coffee

fans who attend Formula One races,
hoping to see a car wreck

pill packaging so tamper-proof that
even the user can't open it

refrozen ice cream

toast crumbs in the butter

Elvis movies

an unreachable back itch

buying the wrong format blades for
    your razor

arriving at the fast-food place a minute
    after the breakfast cutoff time

spending six hours to prepare a meal
    that will take six minutes to con-
    sume

when balding people try to cover it up by combing what's left over the bald spot

irons with a setting for Permanent Press

people who put a new roll of toilet paper on top of the holder

people who imitate some stupid dangerous stunt they saw a fictional character perform

when the waiter asks if you want to smell your wine's bottle cap jabs below the belt

proctologists with big fingers

cheek-pinching relatives

salad bar patrons who touch the food
    with their fingers

falling space junk with unpredictable
    points of impact

when people tell you that your problems aren't as bad as theirs

inveterate punsters who always say
"No pun intended" after making
one

when your mate doesn't close the
bathroom door

that junk-bond king Michael Milken
is still stinking rich

a hard-boiled egg with a semi-liquid
yolk

kids' shoes with laces instead of velcro

becoming too big for your rocking horse

Kermit the Frog, book author

trying to find a rhyme for "orange"

sodium-rich foods

walking past a construction site if you're even vaguely female

that Lassie was male

that India ink comes from China

holidays that are nothing more than excuses for heavy drinking

people who point out problems but offer no solutions

professional complainers

proponents of the metric system

ultra-low-budget science fiction movies

terrorists

people who put cheap wine in fancy
bottles

when chili dogs repeat

pouring soured milk into the last of
the cereal

states having boring, rectangular
shapes, like Wyoming and Colo-
rado

when kids in school buses make rude
gestures at motorists

ring-around-the-collar commercials

bird watchers with binoculars

gaining weight after quitting smoking

becoming famished while watching a
TV cooking show

tugging and pulling at a door like mad
before realizing you should push

that there are only twenty-four hours
in a day

a beautiful picture frame that's just
an inch too small

when the TV shows you loved as a
   child look pretty dumb to you
   now, as an adult

people who constantly ask how much
   things cost you

total denial

idiots who fire guns into the air on
   New Year's Eve

falling asleep before midnight on New
   Year's Eve

sports fans who can recall thousands
   of statistics but forget anniver-
   saries

when the "doctor" is merely a Ph.D.

plumbers' fees

when corny old epigrams all turn out
   to be true

getting a new job and having to
   prove yourself

growing up to become what you decided to be at age eight

making a plop instead of a splash

restrooms with toilet paper dispensers that give you only one sheet at a time

riding in a subway car where someone barfed

when friends become acquaintances

not appreciating what you've got until
it's gone

wearing clothing emblazoned with
free advertising

seeing George Carlin on a wholesome
TV show for children

paying twenty-four dollars for two
ounces of pasta in a trendy restaurant

giving "right" answers, instead of
honest ones

being rated in someone's little black
    book

being laughed *at*, not with

keeping your shoes on all the time

people who frequently say "Huh?"

when your parents turn your old
    room into a shrine

that life is painful, nasty, brutish, and
   too short

overzealous recyclers

people who take life, and themselves,
   too seriously

realizing that a list of things that p*ss
   you off may be found amusing
   by others

that trees had to be killed to make
   this book